TABLE OF CONTENTS

FOREWORD

Do I know what I believe?
Do I believe what I know?
Why do I believe what I believe?
What does that say about me?
Where will my beliefs take me?

These are the questions that have occupied my mind for a long time, but more concentrated recently. They have resulted in this self-examination book of ninety-nine plus one questions directed to help people understand their belief systems and discover who they are. Ninety-nine questions will come from the author and one question will come from the reader. The reader gets to present whatever 'belief' question s/he prefers.

Asking others to share their ideas, thoughts, opinions, comments, feelings and even beliefs is sometimes inviting and easy. A reply may range from a quick "I don't know", to "no comment", to a superfluous answer, to a well-organized, thoughtful, factual and evidenced-based honest response.

Disclaimer: This self-examination book is not intended for debate, or to intimidate, confuse, upset or anger the readers. In fact, it is designed to interest and challenge – in a good way, their belief system nut. The goal is that the readers will really get to know themselves through understanding their belief system nut - after gradually watching the nut open.

My Social Belief System in a Nut

Every society propagandizes its set of cultural mores. These cultural practices of dos and don'ts, rights and wrongs become a natural part of a person's belief system. For however long it remains a part of one's belief system depends upon the person. The person has to examine the information that has been presented. During this personal examination, the questions must then be asked:

- *Do I believe this information to be true or make sense?*

If I say yes to either or both, then the logical follow-up questions would be:

- *Why do I believe this to be true and/or makes sense?*
- *What does that say about me?*

While an alternative question may be:

- *If I do not believe this information to be true and/or make sense, why not?*

an even deeper question may be:

- *Where will my beliefs take me?*

Again, how long it remains a part of one's belief system depends upon the person. So, if the person asks the above questions and decides to believe the information presented to be untrue, and/or does not make sense, therefore adopting a different position; the person then begins to reform and rebuild a new belief system. On 'that' topic; one's belief nut begins to open.

A belief system is like the nut inside of a walnut. The protective shell of the walnut is like the several influences that affect and guard one's beliefs. This self-examination book offers to the active participant (self-examiner) two guarantees:

1. To inform the active participant of how their personal social beliefs are created and sustained.

2. Through questioning both the validity and value of their personal beliefs, to determine both the continued (or discontinued) validity and value to one's personal beliefs.

They will be amazed as their social belief system nut begins to open. They will enjoy the experience of discovering themselves as they critique and rethink both their social belief systems as well as what they thought was their social belief system. The flaws that will be discovered (and we all possess these flaws) will serve as a foundation to one's greater self-awareness, personal development as well as personal _change_.

This book is part of a book series about the belief system. This presentation includes 99 plus 1 questions about social beliefs. This book and all the other future books in this series will be predicated on the following questions: Do I know what I believe? Do I believe what I know? Why do I believe what I believe? What does that say about me? And where will my beliefs take me?

Perhaps the answer to a question may be customized to appeal to the likings of the inquirer. The motivation to appeal to the likings of the inquirer changes when the person asking the question happens to be the same person who will offer and receive the response. Quite naturally, the self-examiner will instantly know the authenticity and depth of his or her response to a question "Do I believe?" A "Do I believe" question does not seek a result of true, false, right or wrong.

When a self-examiner asks the question "Do I believe?" to him or herself, they should immediately know how to respond with conviction: yes, I believe or no, I do not believe. If they have think too long about the "Do I believe?" question, or if they reply that they are not sure, or they do not know what or why they believe, then there is a room for discovery.

That person deserves to know. In fact, perhaps that person would recognize an obligation to know what and why he or she believes or does not believe what the question asks. Additionally, the reader gets to subjectively think about the questions: What does my belief say about me? And where will my beliefs take me?

If the self-examiner takes the next step towards discovering what one believes and why, one's belief system nut will begin to open. One's belief system nut will open even further as one learns the nature of what or who influenced what is believed.

5

You are guaranteed to experience a better understanding about yourself. You'll realize that some of what you truly believe, or even what you thought you believe and why will require rethinking. The rethinking of some of your beliefs may lead to a more informed level of... you.

The practical application of this book provides a platform for group discussions. It is a perfect tool for social retreats or conferences that seek to encourage personal and social transformations. It guarantees to provoke thoughtful discussions about topics that one might argue should not be the concern of the church or government, but rather certain questions are for the individual to resolve.

This book is a must-have for individuals who really want to discover and find themselves. To really know oneself is to know and understand what one believes and to be willing, if necessary, to change those beliefs; especially if a particular belief was created and subsequently sustained by negative influences. Some of the negative influences may include stereotypes, cultural biases, fear, racism, sexism or classism, to name a few.

INTRODUCTION

There is an old adage that states: You are what you believe. The question directed to the reader is: Have you ever taken a moment and given thought to the word believe? What does that mean? Well, according to the Funk & Wagnalls New International Dictionary of the English Language (1995), the word believe means: to accept as true or real.

The word believe in the English language is commonly used in everyday conversations. In other words, it is used as a question or a statement. For instance, one might ask another: Do you believe me? Do you believe that? Can you believe your eyes or your ears? Am I supposed to believe that or you? Or one might say: I just cannot believe you. I do not believe that happened. I cannot believe my eyes or ears. I don't believe I just said nor did that. One might declare: I don't know what, who, when, how or why to believe.

In the past, I often sat alone or would go about my daily occupation and activities and try to make sense of my thoughts and behaviors. In engaging conversations about various topics, I could easily find myself so convicted for what I believe, I was closed-minded. I guess I was like the closed walnut as pictured on the cover of this book. I sometimes selfishly wanted to dominate the conversation, and sometimes I did. I just felt that I knew what I believed and believed what I knew. I held that nothing else mattered, not even if I was right or wrong.

Minutes or days later if I reflected on the dialog, I could begin asking myself about what I really believe versus my temporary thoughts or opinions. I then realized that at times I was equally uniformed and unfit for the conversation because deep down within me I could not satisfy myself to provide answers for what I believe, and what I know, or even why I believe what I believe. I didn't consider the question of what do my beliefs say about me? I was not concerned about where my beliefs will take me. In fact, as I now think about those times, I felt inadequate for my own thoughts and beliefs.

In retrospect of those experiences, coupled with analysis and research, I considered that perhaps I am not alone. So, I wrote this self-examination book that presents 99 plus 1 common questions that other people will find important to ask self, particularly on the topic of their social beliefs.

This book is the key that will help people find and understand who they are. By the way, contrary to popular belief that people should not talk to themselves; actually talking to oneself at times could be healthy. I discovered that in 2010, when I wrote a book titled: Inspire me, speak to my spirit. That book was also a self-examination book. It consisted of inspirational words and phrases that were designed to encourage and empower the reader to simply think, believe and say: "I can", and with confidence, make a plan to do.

So the "make a plan to do" aspect for this present book is to plan to approach this book with an open heart and an open mind, and expect that something new will be discovered about self.

Through the exploration and discovery of one's belief system, one should expect - at minimum to have many questions about what they believe and why or how they come to believe what they believe. They may come to realize that what they believe has meaning and a strong foundation that will never change. Conversely, they may learn that some beliefs have no real value. They may discover that their belief system is tainted with beliefs based on lies, fear, hate, stereotypes, racism, sexism, bigotry, separatism or shear ignorance, to name a few.

The readers may conclude that some beliefs were allowed to exist because they never thought hard enough or sought deep enough with self-questions to understand what they really believe and why they believe what they believe. And the follow- up question of ... and where will my beliefs take me was perhaps never entertained.

This book identifies ten influencers that affect one's beliefs. The influencers include: family, friends, self, culture/customs, education, churches, government, media, businesses and civic organizations.

By the way, these influencers are not restricted to being local. In fact, with more sophisticated communication technologies, global media, social media networks and expanded international travel opportunities the world-over is influenced by well... the world over.

Every belief system's influencers have their own agenda. In other words, every influencer justifies the perpetuation of information as fact and the truth, just and right. The influencers become the creation of one's belief system nut. A belief system is like the nut inside of a walnut. The protective shell of the walnut is like the several influencers that affect and guard one's beliefs. As the active participant engages the exercises in this book, he or she will be amazed as their belief system nut begins to open. They will enjoy the experience of discovering themselves as they critique and rethink their belief systems' flaws.

The 99 plus 1 questions presented in this book are directed to the reader as though the reader is asking self the questions, and looking for understanding. The assumption is that the only person who can offer a response to the questions is the person to whom the direct questions are asked.

Some people will not be comfortable with many of the questions. Some people might get upset or frustrated with the questions. Well, they can only be upset or frustrated with themselves.

The respondent must remember that no one is asking her or him the questions; instead, she or he is asking self the questions. She may choose to answer the questions or she may choose to disregard the questions.

The respondent is able to give thought to each question and not be concerned about a right or wrong, true or false answer. In fact, the questions are designed to be self-serving. The respondent can only be truthful or not truthful to self. No one else can benefit from the answers. The questions are intended to be inquiring and thoughtful.

Some questions can be responded to quickly and with little or no reservation. Conversely, other questions will require deeper and longer thoughts. In fact, to get a better understanding of some of the questions, some of the questions will call for research and or definition of some word terms or topics.

As a self-examination opportunity for the reader; the reader will write her initial response in the "First Response" space provided for each question. There is an additional space, "Second Response" in the book for future follow-up responses to the 99 plus one questions. The book's platform allows the respondent to revisit the questions at a later date. The reader gets to determine when that later date is.

A follow-up response is important, as it allows for a more informed reader. A future revisit to the questions gives the reader an opportunity to think about what he really believes, and why he believes what he believes.

The goal is that he should know what and why he believes and should believe what he knows. A new-found belief might be a result of a major shift in one's belief system. And, as a further result, one's heart and mind may open. Ultimately, this book might be responsible for the reader discovering self.

The reader is encouraged to expound on the questions. However, do not change the original questions. Separate from this book, the reader may vary the original questions in order to create new questions to think about.

The essence of this book will also bring attention to the stereotypes, bigotries, and more that tend to demonize or minimize the value of others. Unspoken fears or personal biases that are rooted in some beliefs may be disclosed.

When we face the crossroads of seeking understanding or the truth through the foundation of what we believe, the essence of our belief systems is brought into question. Sometimes our belief systems will produce evidence of hypocrisy, inconsistency, or contradiction.

"What one believes is absolutely independent of the reality of what is." For example, if I really believe that the snow is coming down outside, and it is not; in fact, outside the sun is shining; my belief has nothing to do with the reality. However, the reality of what is can influence my belief if I accept what I observe as reality.

As I studied this concept for a book, I developed a theory that states: Every belief system has a measure of time before the test and the truth is revealed. For example: Little boy Michael grew up believing that Thomas was his dad. So, Michael's belief is what would be eventually tested. All the while the mother knew Thomas was not the real father of Michael.

When Michael turned eighteen years old and was ready to head off to college, his mother sat him down to tell the truth and break the news to him that Thomas was not his father. She told him the truth. At that point, the measure of time had run its course-when the truth was revealed. When the truth was revealed, Michael's belief system was brought into question. His belief system nut regarding other matters would certainly be brought into question-unavoidably.

This book provides the platform with ninety-nine plus one questions, so that the reader will be able to understand how the test will be applied.

MORE DISCLAIMERS: Some of the questions presented will NOT apply to the reader. In those cases, the respondent may write in the space: DOES NOT APPLY. Some questions may seem to be repeated, but they are not. Some questions may be difficult for some readers to articulate their answers, in those cases, the respondent should do his or her best. Remember, the answers are for the benefit of the reader and no one else.

DEDICATION

This work is firstly dedicated with gratitude to the Almighty God for His infinite wisdom to know my thoughts and beliefs that are deeply rooted in understanding His love for me. I am eternally grateful for the inspiration and courage to write this book that is guaranteed to help people bring into question their belief system nut.

Some people will approach this book with an open mind and a willing spirit; and to their surprise and benefit they will discover themselves. So, in advance, I want to acknowledge and commend those who took advantage of this opportunity to know and understand who they really are. They have ventured to know what they believe and why they believe what they believe and know. They should now have a better idea about where their beliefs came from and where their beliefs will take them. Finally, they should have begun to feel the walnut transform from a closed nut to an open nut.

I love my family, especially my mother Louise and my three young adult children: James Jr., Saunteena, and Semaj. This book has been completed with final touches from Mr. Raymone D. Washington, who has been there for all of the previous fifteen plus books.

SELF-EXAMINATION QUESTIONS INTRODUCTION

The following 99 plus 1 self-examination questions are purposeful. They are designed to provoke and inspire the reader's thoughts about what she or he believes and why. For their information they could have a better sense for where their belief system will take them.

These self-paced questions are guaranteed to challenge the reader's belief system regarding their social beliefs. These questions are designed to inspire and not incite. They are meant to open the heart and mind, and not open a can of worms. They a presented to discover and not discourage. Some questions will really put the reader's knowledge-base to the test. The respondent will find many questions difficult or nearly impossible to answer. These questions, in a way, will serve as a tool to expose the truth, and to establish new discoveries about topics that were never questioned and provided answers, but accepted by default.

The apparent risk to answering these questions is that the respondent will see that some fundamental beliefs will be brought into question. Some respondents will not be comfortable because they will have to make adjustments in their mindset and heart.

Some respondents may become embarrassed because they don't know the answer, or how to answer the simple questions. In fact, some respondents may consider assessing their future actions that pertain to their social beliefs. These questions will serve as an eye-opener. The respondent will find that some of their beliefs just don't make sense. In fact, some might prove to be of no value.

The hope is that, as a personal development benefit, the reader will be encouraged, directed and guided to a better understanding of the many influences that affect their belief system. The hope is also that the respondent will take more personal responsibility to know what is believed and why. After all, we are what we believe, that is, if you believe that.

Before attempting to answer the 99 plus 1 self-examination questions, the reader/respondent should become familiar with the System of Influencers. As the questions are read, begin to think about the different formal or informal influencers that may have influenced and impacted –in a positive or otherwise way what the reader/respondent currently believes. The respondent will have the opportunity to self- examine, as many of the questions ask: "Why do I believe that?, why I do not believe that?"

Another guarantee from this book is that the active reader/respondent will never be the same. Moving forward, the reader/respondent will be sure to scrutinize information they are exposed to before endorsing it and accepting it into their belief system nut. And hopefully the respondent will consider rethinking some things that she believes might lead to a more informed level of beliefs.

NOTE: One's belief system's nut remains intact until it is disturbed by challenging inquiries that seek justification or understanding. So, let's go with the flow.

SYSTEM OF INFLUENCERS
FLOW CHART

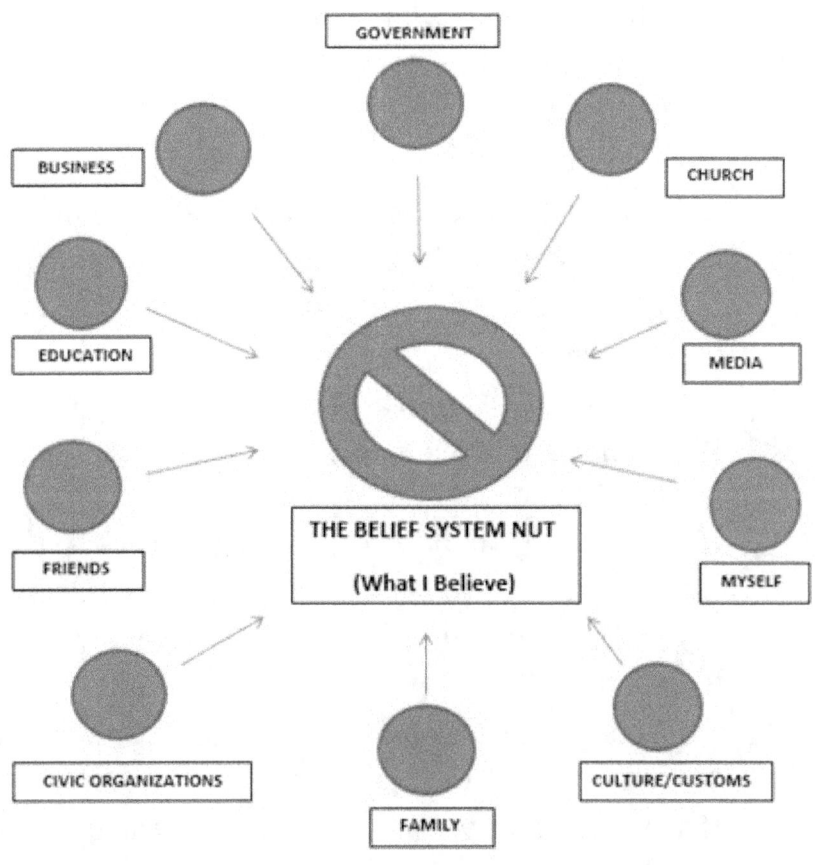

Do I know what I believe?
Do I believe what I know?
Why do I believe what I believe?
What does that say about me?
Where will my beliefs take me?

1. Do I believe I know myself?
2. Do I believe I really know myself?
3. If I believe I really know myself, then who do I believe I am?
4. How do I believe I came to know who I am?
5. If I do not believe I know myself, do I believe I can discover myself?
6. If I believe I can discover myself, what makes me believe that?
7. Do I believe that women should not wear pants?
8. If I believe that women should not wear pants, why do I believe that?
9. If I believe that women should not wear pants, why not?
10. Do I believe it's okay for a women to wear pants to church?
11. Do I believe that women should not wear pants in church?
12. If I believe that women should not wear pants in church, why not?
13. Do I believe that men should not wear earrings?

14. If I believe that men should not wear earrings, why not?

15. Do I believe for a man to wear earrings, it is okay?

16. Do I believe that men should not wear long hair?

17. If I believe that men should not wear long hair, why not?

18. Do I believe that certain colors should be associated with males and females?

19. Do I believe that males should not wear pink clothing?

20. If I believe the males should not wear pink clothing, why do I believe that?

21. Do I believe that females should not play American Football?

22. Do I believe that American Football is meant to be a sport for only men?

23. If I believe that females should not play American Football, why do I believe that?

24. Do I believe that a woman could become the President of the United States?

25. If I believe that a woman could become the President of the United States, why do I believe that?

26. If I believe that a woman could not become the President of the United States, why do I believe that?

27. Do I believe that a woman will become the President of the United States, why do I believe that?

28. If I believe that a woman will not become the President of the United States, why do I believe that?

29. Do I believe that the United States is the best country on earth?

30. If I do I believe that the United States is the best country on earth, why do I believe that?

31. If I do not believe that the United States is the best country on earth, why do I believe that?

32. Do I believe in the existence of UFO's (Unidentified Foreign Objects)?

33. If I believe in the existence of UFO's (Unidentified Foreign Objects), why do I believe that?

34. If I do not believe in the existence of UFO's (Unidentified Foreign Objects), why do I believe that?

35. Do I believe that deadly viruses are man-made?

36. If I do not believe that deadly viruses are man-made, why do I believe that?

37. Do I believe I am knowledgeable about world affairs?

38. If I believe I am knowledgeable about world affairs, what makes me believe that?

39. If I believe I am not knowledgeable about world affairs, what makes me believe that?

40. Do I believe I am knowledgeable about Global Warming?

41. If I believe I am knowledgeable about Global Warming, what makes me believe that?

42. If I believe I am not knowledgeable about Global Warming, what makes me believe that?

43. Do I believe in the existence of Global Warming?

44. Do I believe I know much about the AIDS Virus?

45. If I don't believe I know much about the AIDS Virus, why not?

46. Do I believe there is a hidden cure for the AIDS Virus?

47. If I believe there is a hidden cure for the AIDS Virus, what makes me believe that?

48. If I do not believe there is a hidden cure for the AIDS Virus, what makes me believe that?

49. Do I believe that the AIDS Virus was created by someone?

50. If I believe that the AIDS Virus was created by someone, what makes me believe that?

51. If I do not believe that the AIDS Virus was created by someone, what makes me believe that?

52. Where do I believe the AIDS Virus came from?

53. Do I believe that the "Government" knows more about the AIDS Virus than is reported?

54. If I believe that the "Government" knows more about the AIDS Virus than is reported, why do I believe that?

55. Do I believe that the "Government" has provided all the information available about the AIDS Virus?

56. Do I believe that generally speaking, men are smarter than women?

57. If I believe that generally speaking, men are smarter than women, what makes me believe that?

58. If I believe that generally speaking, men are not smarter than women, what makes me believe that?

59. Do I believe that generally speaking, women are smarter than men?

60. If I believe that generally speaking, women are smarter than men, what makes me believe that?

61. If I believe that generally speaking, women are not smarter than men, what makes me believe that?

62. Do I believe that the death penalty is a good form of punishment?

63. If I believe that the death penalty is a good form of punishment, what makes me believe that?

64. If I believe that the death penalty is not a good form of punishment, what makes me believe that?

65. Do I believe I am safe with the local police?

66. If I believe I am safe with the local police, what makes me believe that?

67. If I believe I am not safe with the local police, what makes me believe that?

68. Do I believe that local government is really concerned about its citizens?

69. If I believe that local government is really concerned about its citizens, what makes me believe that?

70. Do I believe that local government is really not concerned about its citizens?

71. If I believe that local government is really not concerned about its citizens, what makes me believe that?

72. Do I believe that the Republican Party caters more to big business than it does to the Poor?

73. If I believe that the Republican Party caters more to big business than it does to the Poor, what makes me believe that?

74. If I believe that the Republican Party does not cater more to big business than it does to the Poor, what makes me believe that?

75. Do I believe that the Democratic Party caters more to the Poor than to the Rich?

76. If I believe that the Democratic Party caters more to the poor than to the rich, why do I believe that?

77. If I believe that the Democratic Party does not cater more to the poor than to the rich, why do I believe that?

78. Do I believe that abortions are right?

79. If I believe that abortions are right, what makes me believe that?

80. Do I believe that abortion is an individual choice issue?

81. Do I believe that abortions are wrong?

82. If I believe that abortions are wrong, what makes me believe that?

83. Do I believe I know what involuntary manslaughter is?

84. If I believe I know what involuntary manslaughter is, do I believe that one who commits involuntary manslaughter should be punished?

85. If I believe that one who commits involuntary manslaughter should be punished, why do I believe that?

86. If I believe that one who commits involuntary manslaughter should not be punished, why do I believe that?

87. Do I believe that humans are prone to make mistakes?

88. If I believe that humans are prone to make mistakes, what makes me believe that?

89. If I believe that humans are not prone to make mistakes, what makes me believe that?

90. Do I believe that genuine mistakes should be forgiven?

91. If I believe that genuine mistakes should be forgiven, why do I believe that?

92. If I believe that genuine mistakes should not be forgiven, why do I believe that?

93. Do I believe that people who make genuine mistakes should be punished?

94. If I believe that people who make genuine mistakes should be punished, why do I believe that?

95. Do I believe that people who make genuine mistakes should not be punished?

96. If I believe that people who make genuine mistakes should not be punished, why do I believe that?

97. Do I believe that government sponsored programs are designed to fail?

98. If I believe that government sponsored programs are designed to fail, why do I believe that?

99. Do I believe my social belief system nut has opened?

100.(My Question), Why do I believe that?

SELF-EXAMINATION

1. **Do I believe I know myself?**

   Date:

   Date Revisited:

2. **Do I believe I really know myself?**

   Date:

   Date Revisited:

3. **If I believe I really know myself, then who do I believe I am?**

   Date:

   Date Revisited:

4. How do I believe I came to know who I am?

   Date:

   Date Revisited:

5. If I do not believe I know myself, do I believe I can discover myself?
   Date:

   Date Revisited:

6. If I believe I can discover myself, what makes me believe that?

   Date:

   Date Revisited:

7. Do I believe that women should not wear pants?

   Date:

   Date Revisited:

8. If I believe that women should not wear pants, why do I believe that?

   Date:

   Date Revisited:

9. If I believe that women should not wear pants, why not?

   Date:

   Date Revisited:

10. Do I believe it's okay for a women to wear pants to church?
Date:

Date Revisited:

11. Do I believe that women should not wear pants in church?
Date:

Date Revisited:

12. If I believe that women should not wear pants in church, why not?
Date:

Date Revisited:

13. Do I believe that men should not wear earrings?
    Date:

    Date Revisited:

14. If I believe that men should not wear earrings, why not?
    Date:

    Date Revisited:

15. Do I believe for a man to wear earrings, it is okay?
    Date:

    Date Revisited:

16. Do I believe that men should not wear long hair?

   Date:

   Date Revisited:

17. If I believe that men should not wear long hair, why not?

   Date:

   Date Revisited:

18. Do I believe that certain colors should be associated with males and females?

   Date:

   Date Revisited:

19. Do I believe that males should not wear pink clothing?

    Date:

    Date Revisited:

20. If I believe the males should not wear pink clothing, why do I believe that?

    Date:

    Date Revisited:

21. Do I believe that females should not play American Football?

    Date:

    Date Revisited:

22. Do I believe that American Football is meant to be a sport for only men?

Date:

Date Revisited:

23. If I believe that females should not play American Football, why do I believe that?

Date:

Date Revisited:

24. Do I believe that a woman could become the President of the United States?

Date:

Date Revisited:

25. If I believe that a woman could become the President of the United States, why do I believe that?

Date:

Date Revisited:

26. If I believe that a woman could not become the President of the United States, why do I believe that?

Date:

Date Revisited:

27. Do I believe that a woman will become the President of the United States, why do I believe that?

Date:

Date Revisited:

28. If I believe that a woman will not become the President of the United States, why do I believe that?

Date:

Date Revisited:

29. Do I believe that the United States is the best country on earth?

Date:

Date Revisited:

30. If I do I believe that the United States is the best country on earth, why do I believe that?

Date:

Date Revisited:

31. If I do not believe that the United States is the best country on earth, why do I believe that?

Date:

Date Revisited:

32. Do I believe in the existence of UFO's (Unidentified Flying Objects)?

Date:

Date Revisited:

33. If I believe in the existence of UFO's (Unidentified Foreign Objects), why do I believe that?

Date:

Date Revisited:

34. If I do not believe in the existence of UFO's (Unidentified Flying Objects), why do I believe that?

Date:

Date Revisited:

35. Do I believe that deadly viruses are man-made?
Date:

Date Revisited:

36. If I do not believe that deadly viruses are man-made, why do I believe that?

Date:

Date Revisited:

37. Do I believe I am knowledgeable about world affairs?

Date:

Date Revisited:

38. If I believe I am knowledgeable about world affairs, what makes me believe that?

Date:

Date Revisited:

39. If I believe I am not knowledgeable about world affairs, what makes me believe that?

Date:

Date Revisited:

40. Do I believe I am knowledgeable about Global Warming?

Date:

Date Revisited:

41. If I believe I am knowledgeable about Global Warming, what makes me believe that?

Date:

Date Revisited:

42. If I believe I am not knowledgeable about Global Warming, what makes me believe that?

Date:

Date Revisited:

43. Do I believe in the existence of Global Warming?

Date:

Date Revisited:

44. Do I believe I know much about the AIDS Virus?

Date:

Date Revisited:

45. If I don't believe I know much about the AIDS Virus, why not?

Date:

Date Revisited:

46. Do I believe there is a hidden cure for the AIDS Virus?

   Date:

   Date Revisited:

47. If I believe there is a hidden cure for the AIDS Virus, what makes me believe that?

   Date:

   Date Revisited:

48. If I do not believe there is a hidden cure for the AIDS Virus, what makes me believe that?

   Date:

   Date Revisited:

49. Do I believe that the AIDS Virus was created by someone?

    Date:

    Date Revisited:

50. If I believe that the AIDS Virus was created by someone, what makes me believe that?

    Date:

    Date Revisited:

51. If I do not believe that the AIDS Virus was created by someone, what makes me believe that?

    Date:

    Date Revisited:

52. Where do I believe the AIDS Virus came from?
Date:

Date Revisited:

53. Do I believe that the "Government" knows more about the AIDS Virus than is reported?
Date:

Date Revisited:

54. If I believe that the "Government" knows more about the AIDS Virus than is reported, why do I believe that?
Date:

Date Revisited:

55. Do I believe that the "Government" has provided all the information available about the AIDS Virus?

Date:

Date Revisited:

56. Do I believe that generally speaking, men are smarter than women?

Date:

Date Revisited:

57. If I believe that generally speaking, men are smarter than women, what makes me believe that?

Date:

Date Revisited:

58. If I believe that generally speaking, men are not smarter than women, what makes me believe that?

Date:

Date Revisited:

59. Do I believe that generally speaking, women are smarter than men?
Date:

Date Revisited:

60. If I believe that generally speaking, women are smarter than men, what makes me believe that?

Date:

Date Revisited:

61. If I believe that generally speaking, women are not smarter than men, what makes me believe that?

Date:

Date Revisited:

62. Do I believe that the death penalty is a good form of punishment?

Date:

Date Revisited:

63. If I believe that the death penalty is a good form of punishment, what makes me believe that?

Date:

Date Revisited:

64. If I believe that the death penalty is not a good form of punishment, what makes me believe that?

Date:

Date Revisited:

65. Do I believe I am safe with the local police?

Date:

Date Revisited:

66. If I believe I am safe with the local police, what makes me believe that?

Date:

Date Revisited:

67. If I believe I am not safe with the local police, what makes me believe that?
    Date:

    Date Revisited:

68. Do I believe that local government is really concerned about its citizens?
    Date:

    Date Revisited:

69. If I believe that local government is really concerned about its citizens, what makes me believe that?
    Date:

    Date Revisited:

70. Do I believe that local government is really not concerned about its citizens?

Date:

Date Revisited:

71. If I believe that local government is really not concerned about its citizens, what makes me believe that?

Date:

Date Revisited:

72. Do I believe that the Republican Party caters more to big business than it does to the Poor?
Date:

Date Revisited:

73. If I believe that the Republican Party caters more to big business than it does to the Poor, what makes me believe that?

Date:

Date Revisited:

74. If I believe that the Republican Party does not cater more to big business than it does to the Poor, what makes me believe that?

Date:

Date Revisited:

75. Do I believe that the Democratic Party caters more to the Poor than to the Rich?

Date:

Date Revisited:

76. If I believe that the Democratic Party caters more to the Poor than to the Rich, why do I believe that?

Date:

Date Revisited:

77. If I believe that the Democratic Party does not cater more to the Poor than to the Rich, why do I believe that?
Date:

Date Revisited:

78. Do I believe that abortions are right?
Date:

Date Revisited:

79. If I believe that abortions are right, what makes me believe that?

    Date:

    Date Revisited:

80. Do I believe that abortion is an individual choice issue?
    Date:

    Date Revisited:

81. Do I believe that abortions are wrong?
    Date:

    Date Revisited:

82. **If I believe that abortions are wrong, what makes me believe that?**

    Date:

    Date Revisited:

83. **Do I believe I know what involuntary manslaughter is?**

    Date:

    Date Revisited:

84. **If I believe I know what involuntary manslaughter is, do I believe that one who commits involuntary manslaughter should be punished?**

    Date:

    Date Revisited:

85. If I believe that one who commits involuntary manslaughter should be punished, why do I believe that?

Date:

Date Revisited:

86. If I believe that one who commits involuntary manslaughter should not be punished, why do I believe that?

Date:

Date Revisited:

87. Do I believe that humans are prone to make mistakes?

Date:

Date Revisited:

88. If I believe that humans are prone to make mistakes, what makes me believe that?

Date:

Date Revisited:

89. If I believe that humans are not prone to make mistakes, what makes me believe that?

Date:

Date Revisited:

90. Do I believe that genuine mistakes should be forgiven?

Date:

Date Revisited:

91. If I believe that genuine mistakes should be forgiven, why do I believe that?

Date:

Date Revisited:

92. If I believe that genuine mistakes should not be forgiven, why do I believe that?

Date:

Date Revisited:

93. Do I believe that people who make genuine mistakes should be punished?

Date:

Date Revisited:

94. If I believe that people who make genuine mistakes should be punished, why do I believe that?

    Date:

    Date Revisited:

95. Do I believe that people who make genuine mistakes should not be punished?

    Date:

    Date Revisited:

96. If I believe that people who make genuine mistakes should not be punished, why do I believe that?

    Date:

    Date Revisited:

97. Do I believe that government-sponsored programs are designed to fail?

Date:

Date Revisited:

98. If I believe that government-sponsored programs are designed to fail, why do I believe that?

Date:

Date Revisited:

99. Do I believe my social belief system nut has opened?

Date:

Date Revisited:

100.(MY QUESTION)

_____

_____

_____

Why do I believe that?

Date:

Date Revisited:

FINAL THOUGHTS FROM THE AUTHOR

I trust that you, the reader, approached this book with an open mind and a willing spirit. If this is you, then to your surprise and benefit you should have discovered yourself even more than you already knew or thought you knew. Congratulations if you experienced the belief system shift through the 99 plus 1 self-examination questions that you asked yourself, answered and validated. I trust that you probed and probed for answers, and hopefully your belief system is justified. I want to say, *GREAT JOB!*

I want to acknowledge and commend you as you took advantage of this opportunity to know and understand who and why you really are. I hope that you ventured to know what you believe and why you believe what you believe and know. You should now have a better idea about where your beliefs came from and where your beliefs will take you. Finally, you should have begun to feel the walnut transform from a closed to an open nut.

I want to inform you, the reader that everyday new belief system nuts are created and existing belief system nuts are being reinforced. I also want to encourage the you to revisit this book to constantly update the status of your belief system nuts. The ultimate goal is to fully understand your belief system nuts.

THOUGHTS FROM
THE READER

ABOUT THE AUTHOR

Dr. James Edward Bruce, Sr. is a native Bostonian who has a genuine passion for writing. All of his published books are on the themes of the motivational, inspirational and spiritual. This book represents book #20. In particular, it focuses on people's belief systems in relation to their social beliefs. Dr. Bruce enjoys writing books that engage the readers into self-examination. Currently, Dr. James E. Bruce, Sr. is actively supporting several soon-to-be published authors.

Dr. Bruce uses, among his learning and teaching tools, his book #10, titled: "So, You Want to Write a Book; Find Out How". When he wrote and published book #10, he indicated that his goal was to get more people to write and become published authors. He is on a mission.

www.ingramcontent.com/pod-product-compliance
Lightning Source LLC
Chambersburg PA
CBHW071115280526
45787CB00003B/1059